Yorkshire Dales
STONEWALLER

Yorkshire Dales
STONEWALLER

Geoff Lund

Photography by
Geoff Lund

Text by
Richard Muir
and
Maurice Colbeck

Dalesman Books

First published in Great Britain 1992 by Dalesman Publishing Company Limited, Clapham, Lancaster LA2 8EB in association with Curlew Press, an imprint of Timothy Benn Books Limited, 234 Temple Chambers, Temple Avenue, London EC4Y 0DT

Designed by David Harkness

Production by Richard Elgie

Photographs © 1992 Geoff Lund
Text Copyright © 1992 Richard Muir and Maurice Colbeck

British Library Cataloguing - in - Publication Data.
A catalogue record for this book is available from the British Library

ISBN No 1-85568-049-1
Typeset in Palatino by Primary Colours. Colour origination by Primary Colours, London W4.
Printed and Bound by Dai Nippon Printing Co. Ltd.

Contents

THE STONE WALLS OF THE YORKSHIRE DALES

By Richard Muir

1. The Setting

Here in the Yorkshire Dales we find landscapes softly tinted in olive, emerald, brown and silver - and with each piece in the rural patchwork outlined by a thread of stone. In some wild flight of fancy one might imagine that, long ago, a gigantic spider had scuttled across the scene, binding meadow, pasture and common together in a petrified web. Sometimes the web is packed with intricate, winding threads, while in other places it forms a geometry as precise as the lines in a formal garden.

Fields and their walls form the greater part of the scenery of this region – a fact so obvious that most visitors will take it for granted. And so it is easy to forget that each tiny facet of the fieldscape has a reason for being the way that it is, while every single yard of walling embodies a fair amount of thought, sweat and craftsmanship: nobody marked-out a boundary and built a wall simply for the sake of so doing. Perhaps we should also remember that nobody involved in the wearing and often exhausting tasks of quarrying, splitting, hauling, shaping and building would ever spare a thought for the scenic consequences of their efforts. Like all the finest features of the English countryside, the walled fieldscape of the Dales is the result of the struggle to subsist. Concern for the aesthetic aspects was a luxury that the peasant, tenant and shepherd could not afford.

This said, however, it is worth remembering that during a great spate of wall-building in Georgian, Regency and Victorian times there were a few more privileged arbiters of taste about who took a dim view of the changes to the landscape. They mourned the dismemberment of the vast expanses of open common and they loathed the straight-lined geometry of bright walls in fresh-cut stone. A couple of centuries have passed, and the mellowed, lichen-clad walls seem a timeless and essential feature of the landscape. Now, we decry the removal of all dry-stone walls and dread the day when their loss will result in what may be described as featureless prairie vistas. The old walls have shaped our perception of what is right for the the Dales.

It is all very well to ponder on the scenic aspects of the walls, but we must not lose sight of the more basic question of why the walls are there at all?

They were built to divide and to confine; to keep the horn away from the corn; to fold ewes and lambs in the safe precincts of the farmstead; to mark the extent of one tenant's little domain, and generally to partition the farmed landscape into useful little packages. And once built, the walls shielded sheep from the full blast of chilling winds and driving rain, while allowing sufficient draughts from the broken gusts to filter through the chinks in the stones to dry sodden fleeces.

But why walls? After all, in the South and Midlands walls are unusual, and throughout the English lowlands the tasks of dividing and confining are almost entirely accomplished by hedgerows. It is really just a question of convenience. The soft chalks, squelchy clays and crumbly young sandstones of the lowlands are of no interest to the waller, but in the mild and sheltered lowlands the hawthorn can flourish. On the wind-lashed fells and in the sodden high-

The back of
Gordale Scar.
*'This is one of my
favourites, looking
down towards the
crag. It's almost a
miniature Grand
Canyon! I wish I'd
taken it in print,
because it's so
well balanced.'*

er valleys it is a different story. Here the hawthorn may be seen forming patches of scrub, the
gnarled shrubs leaning away from the prevailing
north-westerlies. But it survives rather than
flourishes, and it could never defy the elements
sufficiently to form a dense, sheep-proof hedge.

In the lower and less exposed parts of the
region, however, the thorn hedge has competed
for favour. In the middle sections of Nidderdale,
for example, hedges and walls have proved almost equal in their appeal, while in the cul de sac
of Wensleydale around West Burton there is an
eye-catching stretch of small, hedge-girt fields
which forms an unusual yet appealing contribu-
tion to the scene. It is much more expensive in
cash and effort to build a wall than to plant a
hedge. However, the newly planted hedge re-
quires several years of protection from grazing
before it is established and needs laying about
every 20 years. A well-built wall will endure for
centuries, even if it does need patching in places
from time to time.

To have walls one must first have stone. And
this stone must be cheap; plentiful; tough
enough to resist the rigours of winter, but, pre-
ferably, capable of being split and shaped. In the

Dales, such stone is not only present, it is often
super-abundant. Some of the stones used derive
from the boulders which were painstakingly
clawed from the land as ground was cleared for
cultivation; some were split from the cliffs where
the rocks outcrop in valley-side scars; some
prised from expanses of limestone pavement,
and others hewn from little quarries.

Whatever the particular source of the stone employed, it is always a fairly safe guess that it lay
within a short distance of its wall destination.
Stone is a heavy, bulky and unwieldly commo-
dity, while until quite recent times the routeways
in the Dales were crude in the extreme. Roads
which were sufficiently level, well-graded and
drained as to allow the passage of wheeled transport were very few and far between. The farmer
employed not a wagon but a horse-drawn sledge
to shift materials around his holding, while long-
distance transport was accomplished by hauliers
who used teams of pack ponies. And so it was
prohibitively expensive to move walling stone
across any but the most modest of distances. Fortunately, there was scarcely a locality within the
Dales which could not supply an adequate quality of walling stone – and as a result, the walls of

the region closely reflect the local geology.

The Dales is not the only region in Britain enjoying a distinctive character that is strongly influenced by its drystone walls. In the Cotswolds we find walls of the local honey-gold limestone; in the famous quarrying district of the Isle of Portland there are white walls in a stone so fine that much was shipped away to form some of the capital's grandest buildings, while around Dartmoor, where the local granite is known as 'moorstone', the fields are walled by 'hedges' of intractable boulders wrenched from the ground, heaped together and topped with a crest of shrubs. In the Grampian region there is mile upon mile of walls known as 'consumption dykes': massive field walls built as repositories for the countless thousands of glacial boulders and pebble scoured from the surrounding fields. And similarly, in parts of the Lake District, like the Wasdale Head locality, one can see both thick walls and 'clearance cairns', all serving as dumping grounds for the super-abundant rock debris.

The walls in the Dales are not of a uniform geology; rather, they reflect the contrasts in the underlying rock. These rocks are quite different in their hues and textures, but they are very roughly of the same age and date from the Carboniferous era – the same long period which witnessed the deposition of most of our coal supplies.

More than 300 million years ago, a sagging plain was inundated by the waters of a sub-tropical sea. The part of the earth's crust which was to become the Dales then resembled the Caribbean. The waters were rich in minute aquatic organisms, and as these creatures died, so their limy shells accumulated as a sea-floor sludge. Untold billions of these organisms contributed their skeletons and body armour to the deepening ooze as millions of years passed by. Eventually, the lime deposits were hundreds of feet thick and became compressed into beds of tough, silvery rock which were ultimately uplifted and exposed to form the Carboniferous limestone of the Dales.

As the geological clock ticked on, the conditions around our ancient sea gradually changed. Its margins became shallower. In some places incoming streams deposited layers of mud, in others rivers brought sand, while in others still, forests colonised swampy lagoons and coal deposits formed from the accumulations of fallen timber. All the while, slight rises in the sea level would renew the creation of a limy sea-floor ooze. The enduring result of these fluctuations was the production of alternating bands of rock, with sandstone, shale, coal and limestone occurring in swift succession. When taken together, these rocks are known as the 'Yoredales'.

Once again the conditions for rock formation changed as rivers draining into the Carboniferous sea engaged in a vigorous campaign of erosion against a mountain mass which lay to the

north. Each torrent became charged with a massive cargo of coarse, eroded rock debris, and this debris was dumped to form vast deltas or else swept out across the sea-floor. Meanwhile, the sea-floor sagged and sank under the weight of the accumulating sand. This coarse sand blanket covering the limestone has been uplifted, exposed and eroded, and survives in places as the distinctive Millstone Grit.

The wallers of the Dales have made good use of all these types of stone. Most of the limestone is less tractable than the sandstones and will not readily split into oblong building blocks. Limestone walls are recognised by their more angular and irregular components, as well as by the silvery hue of the rock. In the vicinity of the Yoredales one can expect to find walls which vary in their constituents, with grit, sandstone, limy sandstone and limestone each featuring in the pageant. The grits are the toughest of the sandstones, but after much hammering they can be shaped and squared to produce walls of neatly-coursed and closely-fitting stones. When newly quarried, the grit has a pale buff hue, but following exposure to the elements it darkens to a grey-black tone.

The poverty of the road system played a crucial role in determining that the field walls would harmonise with their setting. Since it was not practical to move stone very far, the walls of local stone, once mellowed by the elements, would al-

Gill above Hubberholme.
'Why is the stream so dry? Because we live in that kind of country, that's why. The river at Litton dries up for three miles. We're living in a porous limestone country and the water sinks into the ground though the cracks.'

ways blend with the surrounding geology. In the limestone country the delicate greys of the stones in the field boundaries echo the hues of the rocks exposed in the scars, pavements and dry streambeds. Gritstone country has a darker, moister and more brooding quality. The parched limestone is full of fissures which divert most surface streams underground, but on the grits a generous tree cover is supported. Moorland develops on the higher, acid soils and ribbons of alder line the river banks. Silvery walls might seem out of place in the more dusky palette of the gritstone landscape, but the dark walls never fail to enhance the scene.

2. The Wallers of Old

Nature provided an abundance of raw materials for walling, but it was man the farmer who discovered the need to mark boundaries and make enclosures. Dalesfolk who have walled their holdings for centuries share a most distinctive culture, albeit one which is now severely threatened by the decay of hill farming and the arrival of vast numbers of 'offcomers'. But one could never regard Dalesfolk as a race. The gene pool of the Dales is a rich mixture of contributions from prehistoric settlers of uncertain origins, from Celts, Anglo-Saxons, Danes and Norsemen, with more modest donations being made by legionaries from all corners of the Roman empire, Norman carpet-baggers, the odd Flemish settler – and who is to say that monks from France and Italy may not have added something to the brew?

Of course, we will never know who first placed one stone on top of another and so began the tradition of walling. Such an event will have occurred as the retreat of the ice sheets on the Pennines made the region more inviting to small bands of hunters, who then moved northwards from the Midlands in pursuit of the herds of reindeer or wild horses. Perhaps the first stones were gathered and set in place to weigh down a tent of hides. But it is very likely that the first coherent piece of walling to be built took the form of a windbreak composed of rubble and boulders stacked together, perhaps to bridge a wind gap in a natural rock outcrop or else to shield a cave mouth camp site from the bitter winds.

If the first tentative and fumbling efforts at walling were attempted in order to secure shelter in the harsh, sub-arctic conditions then prevailing, the gradual improvement in the climate and the eventual adoption of farming lifestyles placed a new and vital emphasis on the ability to work with Nature's building blocks. By quite an early stage during the first age of farming, the people of Britain had developed a remarkable degree of competence in the craft of drystone

walling. This is not so much evident from the relics of fieldwalls as from sections of walling incorporated in the massive megalithic tombs of the New Stone Age. From monuments as far apart as Maes Howe on Orkney and Stoney Littleton in Avon, Bryn-Celli-Ddu on Anglesey and Punds Water on Shetland we find evidence of a degree of accomplishment which modern wallers might envy. Many of these tombs survive in areas which have always been rather impoverished in farming resources – and so it is a little surprising that the rugged countrysides of the Dales are rather poorly endowed in megalithic monuments. Even so, given the nature of traditional farming life, there is no reason to suppose that the ancient drystone wallers of the Dales were any less adept than their counterparts in Wales, Wessex and the Northern Isles.

The patterns of the wall network not only reflect the practical demands of farming, but they also reflect the nature of the society which caused the walls to be built. For example, in any given area the walls built by a community of small, private landowners will form different patterns from those built by a society of peasants who have extensive areas of common pasture, meadow and ploughland. There are several places in the Dales where three or four quite distinct and different efforts at partitioning the countryside are evidenced by superimposed patterns of walls, some of the walls being redundant fossils of the fieldscape while others are still well-maintained and useful. Georgian and Victorian walls can be seen cutting across the network of medieval boundaries, while these in turn are superimposed upon the tumbled and overgrown rubble of Iron Age walling. Each society had its own particular ideas about the best way to partition the localities. The little and roughly rectangular enclosures of the Iron Age reflect a very different approach to farming life when compared to the larger, geometrical fields of the 18th-century. Some efforts at division were fairly short-lived, though in places the early medieval boundary walls of Fountains Abbey still play an active part in the pattern of farming.

To explore the earliest known examples of field walls in the British Isles we must look beyond the region of the Dales to places like the southwest of England and the west of Ireland. One might imagine that the oldest known examples of walling would represent rather piecemeal and artless attempts to protect small woodland clearings from the browsing animals of the wildwood. Instead, however, we encounter extensive networks of walled fields which seem to reflect far-reaching and highly organised efforts to partition the countryside into useful packages. The oldest networks were discovered in Co Mayo on the moist Atlantic margins of Europe, where the ancient fields were sealed and blanketed by an ever-deepening layer of peat long before the pre-

historic period had run its course.

Archaeologists learned that local farmers had set up an illicit whiskey still within a tomb of the New Stone Age, which had been discovered during peat digging work. During the early 1960s they excavated the tomb, which they dated to the period around 3000 BC, and they realised that ancient field walls were radiating outwards from this tomb. As the peat was stripped away, walls were revealed which showed that the locality had been divided into fields, each of around 6 acres (2.4 hectares) in area. Elsewhere in Co Mayo, peat-stripping revealed stone walled field networks with fields which were 3 to 4 acres in area. These patterns of fairly rectangular fields had a surprisingly modern appearance and revealed that the Stone Age farmers had already tamed and mastered their setting.

This impression is reinforced by the great tracts of Bronze Age fields which have been recognised on Dartmoor, another region where the impoverishment of the environment by an advancing carpet of peat had protected the ancient patterns against destruction by later generations of farmers. The walls, known locally as 'reaves', appear to result from a single great decision to reorganise the pattern of farming on Dartmoor which was taken around 1700-1600 BC. They were built as banks of boulders and earth, which may originally have been crowned by hedgerows. In some places the reaves were set out along lines which were previously marked by fences. The reave patterns reveal boundaries marking out blocks of countryside, with each block being subdivided into scores of walled fields. Each of the communities living around the moor was provided with grazing on the moorland commons, enclosed fields on the sloping ground and also valley bottom land. The reaves form coherent patterns covering thousands of acres of countryside and well over 125 miles of these ancient walls have been recognised and much more must await discovery. We are not encountering haphazard Bronze Age attempts to enclose small pockets of countryside. Rather, we discover a great campaign to parcel-out land on a vast scale, one which not only created clearly defined territories for the neighbouring moorland communities, but which also sub-divided these territories into detailed and coherent field patterns. Given the scale of the operations, it was inevitable that the building of the walls was not accomplished by individual peasants working in isolation but by gangs of labourers engaged in building one long stretch of reaves after another.

To discover the succession of old walling opera-

Walls below Kettlewell. *'I was asked to take this one, off the Kettlewell road, to show the amount of walls that were allotted each field to each farmer. It's a marvellous pattern.'*

tions in a setting not too different from that of the Yorkshire Dales we must move to Derbyshire, where fascinating work was carried out by Martin Wildgoose between 1978 and 1986 for his Roystone Grange Project. From a close and expert scrutiny of the countryside he was able to recognise several distinct periods of wall-building. At Sheldon near Bakewell, just beyond his study area, a short section of walling dating back to before the introduction of farming (which took place around 5000 BC) has been discovered. It represents a rock shelter which was built to shield a hunter-gatherer band in the Middle Stone Age. Some of the prehistoric walls discovered at Roystone Grange may date back to the dawn of farming and now consist of short lengths of walling by stones set end to end which thus link-up natural outcrops of rock.

Surviving far better than the prehistoric walls of the area are those which were built by the native farmers of the locality during the years of the Roman occupation. These walls are massive and were built in a distinctive manner. The main structure of the wall was provided by a double row of 'orthostats', large, angular boulders. The space in the core of the wall between the two rows of boulders was then packed by rubble, while smaller boulders were set in rows as facings at the base of the orthostats on either side of the wall. These walls, often seeming to date from the 2nd-century AD, will have been somewhat more elaborate and bulky than the walls

which were built at Roystone Grange during the Middle Ages, a thousand years later. In the years around 1200 AD walls were built which consisted of a single row of large, unshaped boulders upon which smaller stones were balanced. Though full of gaps and rather rickety in appearance, such walls could have been effective means of containing sheep, the animals being reluctant to leap or scale a structure which looked likely to collapse upon them.

Walls built at Roystone Grange during the 16th- and 17th-centuries had a much more modern appearance. Like the walls which were built in profusion during the 19th-century, these walls consisted of double rows of stones, stones which diminished in size as the height of the wall increased so that each side of the wall sloped slightly inwards to the point where the top of the wall was sufficiently narrow to be bridged by a single topstone. Walls of both ages also incorporate 'through' stones which run from one side of the wall to the other and help to bind them together. However, the stones used in the 16th- and 17th-century walls were more angular than those used in the later walls and the voids between the two stone rows were not filled by a packing of stone chippings. Unlike the 19th- century walls, those of the 16th- and 17th-centuries were built directly upon the land surface rather than having their foundations set in a shallow trench.

Less is known about the history of walling in the Yorkshire Dales, though it is plain that a wealth of fascinating discoveries await the archaeologist. Prehistoric walls can be seen in a variety of places, notably on the old commons above Grassington and on the high pasture below the summit of Addlebrough. The massive, angular, limestone orthostats which were hauled and rolled to provide the footings for the Grassington walls are still exposed, and vantage points can be exploited to observe the full sweep of the network of small, walled fields. The ancient enclosures, droveways and ruined dwellings tell of an upland countryside which was carefully tended and well-peopled. Now it is rabbit-ridden and exists only as poorer pasture. The ancient fields of the Yorkshire Dales have been attributed to the late-Iron Age and Roman periods. However, firm dating evidence has not always been available and the systems of ancient fields currently being explored around Reeth in Swaledale have echoes of the Dartmoor reaves and might be of the same great antiquity.

Late in the prehistoric period, walling on a gigantic scale was accomplished to fortify the summit of Ingleborough. This was the loftiest of England's hillforts, and one of the most imposing. The flat and wind-blasted hilltop was defended by a stone rampart built to enclose a pear-shaped area measuring around 360 yards by 250 yards. About 20 stone-walled dwellings were erected inside these ramparts, but it is im-

Below Scargill. Some call it Upper Wharfedale: Geoff calls it Kettlewelldale, an older term perhaps. *'That eroded limestone is beautiful, and there's just a smatterin' of snow.'*

possible to imagine that a community could have endured here during the long, harsh months of winter. The rampart, around 13 feet thick, was built of Millstone Grit rubble gathered from the summit rock fields and quarried from scoops around the fort. Its inner face was composed of massive orthostat blocks, while the outer face was of drystone walling. In order to stabilise the mass of rubble, lines of upright stone slabs were built through the wall every six feet or so to compartmentalise the structure.

Some sections of the rampart have been lost completely, but in the north-east angle the drystone walling still stands 5 or 6 courses high. Though the exact date of the building of the hillfort is not known, it existed as a major stronghold and political capital of the Brigantes tribe, a warlike and turbulent federation which dominated the northern hill country in late-Iron Age and Roman times. It is sad that their monument on Ingleborough is slowly being reduced by walkers who gather stones from the rampart and ruined dwellings and add them to the useless summit cairns.

3. Walls for Different Tasks

Drystone walls have always been a functional part of the Dales countryside. Over the passing centuries the patterns which they form across pasture and ploughland have changed in tandem with the changes in farming practices. Such changes were inevitable, for the walls were just an expression of the farmers' needs.

The ancient walls of Swaledale and the Iron Age and Roman walls which can be traced elsewhere are fossils of a countryside divided into an intricate patchwork of small, rather rectangular fields. Most of these fields will have existed as pastures for most of the time, but on the deeper and more sheltered soils some fields will periodically have been tilled to yield a grain crop. The outlines of this pattern may have been preserved into Dark Age times, but then the shock waves from a revolutionary new system of farming which had transformed much of the Midlands began to have some effect in the Dales.

In many parts of the Midlands the old hedgerows were grubbed-up to create the vast expanses of ploughland associated with open field farming. New villages swelled at the heart of each local farming empire, the arable land was divided between a few enormous fields, the fields were divided into blocks or furlongs and the furlongs in turn were divided into dozens of ribbon-like plough strips. In the Dales the areas suitable for cultivation were much more limited in their extents and the new villages fewer, smaller and further between. And so although open field farming did become established here,

its impact was more localised and the scale of the operations was reduced. Wherever the new system was adopted, the old field divisions must have been swept away and the only walls or hedges then used may have been those which defined the main divisions in the landscape of farming: the pastures, woodland, meadows, common and arable fields.

The medieval countryside had a much more open or prairie-like appearance, for one great network of hedges and walls had been destroyed and another was yet to be built. At the same time, there was still a need to divide and confine, with walls, banks and ditches or hedges being employed in different places at different times. Around the village dwellings, individually-held closes or small fields were often found, while barriers were essential to keep the village livestock out of the common meadows and common ploughlands. At Linton in Wharfedale, the medieval walls which protected the open ploughlands of the village still stand. In many of the Dales the pattern of land-holding was a jigsaw of feudal farming, monastic estates and royal and aristocratic hunting grounds. Disputes between the rival interests were rife and boundaries had to be defined and marked on the ground.

Where the potential ploughland was too limited to allow the adoption of an open field farming system on the Midlands model, the folk of the Dales hamlets employed an in-field out-field arrangement. A pocket of the best land was heavily manured and kept in constant production as the communal in-field, while sections of the surrounding out-field were periodically tilled, worked to exhaustion and then aban-

Starbotton. *'I took it because of that big, beautiful natural limestone wall. Whoever built it just picked the stones up and put 'em there, they didn't organise them. They put 'em there to stop cows going over. In the olden days there were warble flies about and they would attack a cow's hind leg. The cow would come tearing down the hill and that line of rocks would deter it and prevent it going over the edge.'*

doned for several years until some fertility returned. Here too it was essential to employ a barrier to keep the cattle and sheep apart from the growing crops.

As time passed by, so the nature of landholding evolved. Originally, the peasants had tenanted strips of ploughland and had balloted for shares or doles in the meadow – all of which were widely scattered. Increasingly, the ambitious villagers wanted to control compact blocks of land and do away with the time-wasting journeys between the fragments of their scattered holdings. This could often be achieved by agreements between village neighbours, who swapped and sold their strips, so that gradually the old patterns of open field farming were dismembered. After the close of the Middle Ages, the pace of the assault on the seemingly out-moded patterns of feudal farming increased. At Grassington, for example, the lord of the manor, the Earl of Cumberland, raised some ready cash in 1603 by selling short leases to his tenants. They began to dismantle the strip patterns in the village West Field. Fields were formed from bundles of adjacent strips and were surrounded by walls. These small, elongated fields still survive in the countryside under a mile to the north-west of Grassington. As at so many other localities in the Dales, the slightly curving walls preserve the 'reversed S' outlines of old strip margins. It is said that such curving forms were produced by the need to begin to swing the plough team well before the headland was reached.

One feature of the decay of feudal farming was the increase in the number of privately tenanted closes surrounding the villages. These little fields, ideal for supporting a horse, ox or the family milk cow, had walls which were sometimes built upon footings formed of massive boulders levered from the land nearby. Away from the village, fields of a different kind were being created as the farmers enclosed land at the lower margins of the ancient commons. These 'intakes' are recurrent and distinctive features of the countryside. The pattern probably began to develop at quite an early stage during the Middle Ages and it continued to expand for two or three centuries after that period had closed. Intaking often hovered in the borderlands of legality. Frequently, peasant families would alienate a patch of land from the open common or waste, while their lords, faced with intaking on almost every front, would judge it more convenient to take a rent for the encroachments rather than attempt to turn the tide. Over the centuries, the piecemeal privatisation of community land produced a zone of irregular, walled intakes in the zone between the village meadows, pastures, ploughlands and closes on the one side and the surviving expanses of common where the beasts of the local farmers still roamed together on the other.

Throughout the Dales, intakes of varying dates form an important part of the fieldscape. The networks marked by walls in Wensleydale around Askrigg, on the high valley slopes in the upper section of Swaledale or the scenes around Stainforth are just a few which come to mind. In the case of Grassington, where the intakes lie between the Iron Age field patterns and those which resulted from the enclosure of the medieval field strips, the origins are a little unusual. These irregular fields were created during the Middle Ages by peasants who enclosed land not for pasture, but to grow coppiced hazel trees. They needed a supply of light timber because they were deprived of access to the manorial woodland in Grass Wood. Intaking continued long after this, and right up to the formal enclosure of the old Forest of Knaresborough in Nidderdale, late in the 18th-century, the official records are packed with complaints about illegal squatting and land-grabbing on the margins of the Forest commons. The walls of the intakes which were created during the two centuries following the close of the Middle Ages vary in appearance. Most were built without resort to expert wallers and some have a very bulky and massive appearance. This results from the walls being built not only as boundary-markers and barriers, but also as convenient repositories for the mass of stones gathered from the newly-enclosed fields.

The pace of enclosure and walling had gradually increased during Tudor, Elizabethan, Jacobean and Commonwealth times, but it was utterly outstripped by the frantic activity which took place during the Georgian and early-Victorian eras. So much of the fieldscape of the Dales is not part of an ancient countryside, but rather a legacy of the 18th- and early-19th centuries, as I shall later describe.

4. Features of the Walls

Few walls continue for great distances before gaps of one kind or another are encountered. Such gaps were needed to allow flocks of sheep to pass from one enclosure to the next, to allow rambler or workman to move through the countryside without engaging in damaging attempts to scale the walls, or to allow ponydrawn tumbrils or sledges to negotiate the network. The need to breach the networks produced 'wall furniture' in the form of gates, gateposts, stiles and 'cripple holes'. In addition the wall pattern often included small pens, essential to the task of tending and sorting the flock.

Sheep creeps, known locally as 'cripple holes' and 'smout holes', are rectangular openings which are just large enough to allow a sheep to pass from one pasture to the next. Where a cripple hole is still being used, one will find a boulder or slab beside it, one which is large enough to block the gap and so confine the sheep, yet light enough to be moved aside to let them pass. Studies in Derbyshire seem to show that the creeps built during the 19th-century are twice as high as they are wide, while those created during the earlier ages of wall building were more roughly built and had square openings. Invariably, a hefty slab of stone is used to serve as a lintel which must bear the weight of the wall stones above the opening, while the jambs or sides of the creep are of carefully coursed stones which carry the ends of the lintel. Much less commonly seen are cow creeps. Here the lintel can be removed to let a cow pass from one pasture to the next and the wall stones above the lintel are crudely piled together and must be removed and then replaced each time that the beasts are moved. With so much dismantling and reconstruction being involved, it is not surprising that most cattle farmers considered it prudent to invest in gates rather than cow creeps!

Stiles take the form of steps or of squeezes or combinations of the two types. Steps are created by setting robust, slab-like through stones in the wall at intervals so that they project from it to form steps like the treads in a staircase. The weight of the stones above these throughs must be sufficient to prevent them from acting like levers to prise the wall apart under the weight of a heavy man. Stiles such as this have been noted in walls of a medieval date. Alternatively, some wallers would build 'heads' or well-made wall ends around a couple of feet apart and then set slender stone pillars or 'stoops' against each head. This was done in such a way that the remaining gap was too narrow near ground level to allow a sheep to squeeze through, but above knee height the gap gradually broadened to allow a walker to pass through. Sometimes the two techniques were combined, so that the lower level of the stile was formed by steps which then rose to a gap in the upper half of the wall.

In the lowlands the five-bar field gates of oak were carried on heavy, oaken gate-posts. In the

Stile at Gayle on the path to Hawes church. *'I could have made that better if I'd had a step-ladder with me – that would have brought the church down and I'd have got more of Hawes. Look at that yellow lichen on the stile.'*

ed or hedged pounds or pinfolds.

There the lord's pinder would impound any stock found straying in the neighbouring fields, the animals being kept in custody until their owners had settled the consequent fine. Other little pens and paddocks have always been essential to the sorting and treating of sheep. Some were needed to sort-out animals when the village flock from the common was rounded-up and others were used by the individual farmer, who needed to confine and catch sheep that required washing or treatment for foot rot and other ailments. Small walled pens can be recognised among the fossilised fields of the Iron Age or found inter-mixed with the dwellings at ancient hamlets – like the Roman native settlement of Ewe Close, between the Pennines and the Lake District, near Crosby Ravensworth.

5. Building the Walls

In many parts of the Dales, particularly on the higher ground, most of the walling dates from the 18th- and early-19th centuries. Although a variety of different methods of wall-building had been employed during the preceding centuries, it is plain that by this time an extremely effective system had been developed. It allowed the construction of walls which were excellent in every respect, which were quite similar to those built by modern wallers and which required no mortar.

Although there is ample evidence for the use of field walls in the Iron Age, in the millennium which followed, thorn hedges seem to have been preferred to drystone walls. As already pointed out, there are plenty of places in the Dales where hedging thorns cannot flourish, but during the Middle Ages the higher, more exposed ground existed as open common and was not subdivided. The old documents for the manors of Wakefield and Bradford show that walls were often used for enclosing house and garden plots, but that hedges were generally favoured as field boundaries.

How then did the walling skills which were so expertly employed in Georgian and Victorian times accrue? It seems clear that this craft of drystone walling must have developed between the later stages of the Middle Ages and the launching of the great enclosure movement. The gathering of skills must have gained momentum during the 17th-century, for it was at this time that walls were very frequently being built to enclose land which had passed into private tenancy during the decay of the old village open field lands. The Derbyshire evidence supports this notion, and we have seen that the walls of this period resembled those of the following centuries, the principal difference being the failure to pack the

Old gate at Howgill Lodge.
'Those are pine branches just slotted in. There's a hole in one gatepost and a slot in the other. It's a marvellous gate. The fence it was in has gone now. I built the wall behind it.'

Dales, however, the gateposts are of stone. All manner of interesting antiquities were liable to be commandeered for humbler duties, and Roman milestones, Saxon crosses and ornate fragments of monastic masonry were all redeployed by the farmer. More usually, roughly-shaped gateposts of gritstone were obtained, with holes being drilled to take the bolts of the hinges; sometimes molten metal was poured into secure the hinge in its socket. In gates of an old design, only the top was carried on a hinge, while below, the foot of the gate carried a peg which was slotted into a socket stone lying partly buried in the ground. When such gates were being hung, the socket stone could be moved until the gate was finely balanced to swing gently closed when released.

Small walled enclosures or pens are an essential feature of hill farming country and they are known by a variety of names, like the 'fanks' of the west of Scotland and the 'stells' of the eastern border country. The old monastic documents tell of large folds being created for sheep during the Middle Ages. Sometimes built to accommodate flocks of 200 or more sheep, these monastic folds seem most commonly to have been hedged and ditched or fenced rather than walled, and they often seem to have been associated with sheep houses where the animals could winter on lower, more sheltered ground. Sheep dung was a most valuable fertiliser and often the medieval farmland was temporarily divided by portable hurdles. These allowed sheep to be penned on a particular patch of ground which was in need of enrichment. In medieval and later times the more populous of the townships had small wall-core of the wall with fillings. It was also around this time that walls came to be preferred to hedgerows, and one must strongly suspect that many of the existing hedgerows were replaced by walls rather than being replanted or revitalised by laying.

The fruit of all this activity and evolution was a wall of a design which was engineered to have the strength to resist the blasting winds and the clambering, scrabbling sheep. Its structure was such that the different parts of the wall helped to support each other, the stones meshing together for mutual support.

The first stage in building a drystone wall involves marking its line upon the ground. Most of those made during the 18th- and 19th-centuries were set-out precisely according to a detailed plan and were uncompromisingly straight. Those of the earlier centuries would tend to curve and waver according to the eccentricities of the terrain. Once the line of the wall was marked out on the ground then turf and topsoil were removed to create a shallow trench around 40 to 50 inches wide which would accommodate the stones selected for the footings of the wall. These were large stones which had at least one fairly level face or 'end'. They were positioned in a double row with their ends facing outwards. Each stone was carefully bedded on the subsoil to ensure that the footings of the wall were firm and stable, and any hump-backed tops were scrappelled away with a mason's hammer so that the next row of stones would bed closely upon the footings. Then the gap between the parallel rows of footings was filled with rough, angular stone chippings or 'fillings', ranging in size from that of a fist to that of a walnut. In the best-made walls each chip of stone was individually placed so that their edges and corners would grip together as the wall rose.

With the footings in place, successive courses of stone were built. The degree to which the wall could be neatly coursed would depend partly upon the skill of the waller concerned and partly upon the nature of the stone being employed. Coarse sandstone, like the Millstone Grit, can, if time permits, be scappled to produce rectangular blocks, and neatly-squared-and-coursed gritstone walling can be seen on the roadside boundaries of many estates. Other stones, like some limestones, would only allow the most basic shaping efforts, and where they are used then the rough coursing is regularly interrupted to accommodate stones of an irregular character. The more angular and uncompromising the stone then the greater the skill demanded of the waller.

In positioning each stone the waller sought to have a fairly level end forming part of the outer face of the wall. But it was even more important that the top of each stone should be as horizontal as possible in order to provide a level bed for the stone which would be placed above. Stones which dipped outwards were sometimes said to assist the drainage of the wall, while an inward dip made it easier to build a wall with a 'batter' – yet the best wallers always aimed to keep the tops of their courses horizontal throughout. The batter of the wall was an upward taper which resulted in walls which became progressively narrower as they rose in height. It was achieved by setting the ends of the stones in each course very slightly back from the ends in the course below.

As the double rows of stone in each course were set in place, so the gaps between them were packed with fillings. But periodically the pattern was broken to allow a 'through' to be incorporated. These are stones built into the wall with their long axes running right through it to link the parallel courses together by spanning the full

width. The waller began to incorporate throughs at intervals when the courses had risen to above knee height, with a second course which included through stones being built when the wall was around chest high. Sometimes in the tallest walls throughs were also included to run through the uppermost of the double rows. Through stones were used in this way to bind the two wall faces together, preventing one face from bulging away from the other, which would cause the wall to slump.

As walling progressed, the waller would tend to select the largest stones from his pile, the degree to which each stone required scappling depending upon its angularity. In this way the courses would tend to narrow with increasing height. The method of building with a batter also ensured that the wall narrowed in width as it

Wall at Grimwith reservoir. *'The walling was done by groups of people. It's a good piece of walling, but if you notice, some of the tops are put on with cement.'*

rose, so that when the chosen height was reached, the top of the wall was sufficiently narrow to be bridged by a single row of topstones. A wall with a full height of six feet will generally be about three feet wide at its base and will taper evenly to a width of around 15 or 16 inches at the base of the top stones.

Before the topstones were set in place a good, flat bed had to be prepared. Sometimes it was necessary to use slender fragments of flagstone to level-up the bed. Alternatively, the topstones were sometimes bedded in lime mortar and mortared together. This prevented leaping sheep or thoughtless ramblers from beginning the destruction of a length of wall by knocking-off topstones, but mortar will not give with any slight movement in the wall, so that drystone methods were preferred. Often, the topstones or capstones were set so that they leaned slightly against each other and all tipped in one direction, perhaps with a more massive topstone being incorporated in a convenient place to bear the weight of its leaning neighbours. The degree to which topstones are shaped varies considerably from wall to wall. All should have well-levelled bases; some are only roughly rounded to a half-oval profile, others very neatly smoothed, while topstones with a triangular profile are quite frequently seen. Less commonly seen is the saw-tooth 'buck and doe' pattern of alternating tall and short topstones and the variant of a tall stone being set after two, three or four low ones have been placed.

The waller accomplished his work using only the most basic set of tools. String lines marked the orientation and the intended height of the wall, while a simple wooden template was often used to test its cross section. Picks and spades were used to dig-out the foundation trench, while the shaping of stones was done with a mason's hammer weighing three or four pounds.

The wallers themselves had a variety of backgrounds. Some were full-time professional dykers, some local rough masons who were as happy building a laithe or repairing a bridge, while others still were farmers who had acquired the rudiments of the skill as an essential adjunct to life in the hill country. A competent waller would expect to complete a six or seven yard stretch of wall in the course of a day's work.

The terminology and the details of the craft varied from region to region. In the Cotswolds, where most walls built from narrow slabs of the easily-worked local limestone were but 20 inches wide and often only three feet tall, the topstones were known as 'combers' and the throughs as 'ties'.

Abandonded millstone on Plover Hill under Pen-y-ghent.
'They must have been carving this when production suddenly ceased and they just left it where it was. Perhaps the market had ceased. At a guess, I'd say it would weigh six or seven hundredweights. How they got that hole through the middle I haven't a clue. I can't see how they could chisel it out – it's too precise. They must have had some sort of a steam-powered drill. It's almost like a bore-hole. The date? Early nineteenth century, would you say?'

6. The Great Enclosure

In the centuries leading up to the Georgian era, land in the Dales had been enclosed with walls in a rather piecemeal fashion. Most of the shorter walls were built to surround packets of private property, many of which resulted from the dismantling of the feudal patchwork of common ploughland, meadow and pasture. Where long walls were built to mark the limits of communal resources, like the common, or to define the boundary between the townships then the elected Bylawman of the township would require all the commoners of that township to take part in the building or repair of the walls. But there were still great expanses of open strip fields, while in parish after parish the vast commons spread like open ranges across the rough grazings and peaty moors of the fells.

The event which signalled the destiny of the landscape in the Dales occurred unheralded and far away, and scarcely a soul living in the Dales will even have heard about it – while any who had will have died before it had any impact upon the farming communities of these northern valleys. In 1604 Parliament passed an Act for the enclosure of the parish of Radipole in Dorset. It involved a systematic privatisation of the common land, with each local landowner receiving a compact grant of land which was notionally equivalent to his or her share in the village public land resources prior to enclosure.

By the time that the last enclosure Act was passed in 1914, thousands of English localities had been transformed. Between 1700 and the outbreak of the First World War around 5,400 Acts were passed, affecting some 7 million acres of communal land. And yet the potential of the events at Radipole was slow to be recognised, for only around 200 parishes were affected in the first half of the 18th-century, the enclosure movement exerting its greatest effects in the century following 1750. Throughout the English lowlands the privatisation of the countryside was expressed in the planting of over a billion thorn saplings to make about 200,000 miles of new hedgerow. In the Dales, however, the length of new walling was several times that of the new hedgerows there, and as we have seen, the farmers, rough masons and dykers had already developed a method of walling which was extremely robust and effective.

The effect of privatisation, then as now, was to benefit the rich and impoverish the poor for, although the principles of enclosure seemed equitable, in practice it tolled the deathknell for the English peasant and sent a stream of broken commoners flooding from the land. Enclosure was set in motion when the leading landowners in a parish petitioned Parliament for an Act of Enclosure. This would almost invariably be given, even when the owners of the majority of land were few in number and greatly outnumbered by smallholders and tenants who had every reason to dread the changes. Parliament having obliged, commissioners were then appointed to oversee the award, normally local worthies such as the squire, parson and a leading freeholder. Meanwhile, the threatened lesser lights of the farming community would often hold anti-enclosure meetings in the locality, passionately expressing their fears – though to no avail. The commissioners would appoint a surveyor and a valuer and these specialists were responsible for measuring and assessing each holding in the existing order of things and for producing a blueprint for the new, privatised arrangement. In theory, the jigsaw of field strips would be disentangled, the common sliced-up and at the end of the day each landholder would obtain a compact holding which was equivalent

to the fragmented share of communal resources.

The surveyor's map of the new parochial world of landownership was then transferred to the countryside itself. Surveyors dealt in straightline geometry. There was no allowance in their arithmetic for subtle curves or for concessions to the undulations and eccentricities of the terrain. Once ruled on the map a line must then be superimposed upon the landscape without regard to knoll or bog.

The enclosure movement embodied both a spirit of agricultural reform and a contempt for the poorer members of country society. The progressive landowner of substance found it very difficult to introduce new crops and methods of cultivation when his holding was in scattered strips which were locked into the old rotations which the community operated in the fields and furlongs. And he found it unrewarding to attempt to improve the pedigrees of his sheep and cattle when they were set free to wander with the mongrels of the village flock and herd on the open fell. Among the farming cogniscenti there was a general contempt for the system of open field farming – though nobody attempted to explain why, if it was really so inefficient, it had endured in places for a thousand years.

Those who had plenty and those who had just a little made common cause against the rural poor, who had next to nothing. Perhaps this was a way of masking guilt or of bolstering status. Com-

At Howgill Lodge – a wall that Geoff built.
'It's eight to nine feet high. To build a new wall here higher than six feet today you'd need permission from the National Park.'

moners who had no stake in the land of the parish other than rights to the common were the favourite target. Robert Stockdale of Knaresborough expressed the contempt and prejudice of many when he wrote that the common "... afforded their families a little milk, yet they would attempt to keep a horse, and a flock of sheep. The first enabled them to stroll about the country in idleness, and the second, in the course of every three of four years, were so reduced by the rot, and other disasters, that on the whole they yielded no profit."

Enclosure got rid of the squatters and cottagers of the common, for they were deemed to have no rights in the share-out. The next to go were the farmers of the smaller kind. Firstly, the compacted holding which they received under the award could in no way compensate for the loss of rights to the common. It had provided not only grazing, but also fuel, bedding and had satisfied several other crucial little needs. Secondly, while the big farmer could meet the costs of enclosure, involving the building of walls or planting of hedges, plenty of smaller men could not afford to carryout the specified work. And so, in parish after parish throughout the Dales, the aftermath of Parliamentary enclosure involved a great exodus of Dalesmen as the broken cottagers and smallholders left their ancestral homelands. Some looked for work in the lead mines; some trekked

southwards to the fastly erupting mill towns, while others still said farewell to the land that had treated them so badly at Liverpool docks.

For those for whom the fruits of enclosure had a less bitter taste there was urgent work to be done. The commissioners were responsible for ensuring that the introduction of the new order was brought to a speedy and effective conclusion. Either they gave a precise specification for the size and construction of new walls – which were to be built within a brief timespan – or else they actually employed contractors to build walls at the expense of those who had obtained land under the award. In any event, it was ensured that the lines on the surveyor's map were translated into drystone courses, for the commissioners could hire dykers to wall any unfenced holding and then take a rent from the land concerned until the debt had been defrayed.

Suddenly there was an exploding demand for walls and wallers in the Dales. In former times walling had been done by individual farmers and by township gang labour recruited by the Bylawmen. Now, however, the scale of the work, the urgency of the timescale and the strict quality controls made it impossible for all the work to be accomplished within the community. Professional help was needed, and just as the peasants evicted from the land were looking for work in the lead mines so some miners found safer employment on the land. They already had skills in breaking rock and shoring-up shafts. In fact the region was full of men who had stitched together a livelihood from bits and pieces of part-time work in mining, smallholding and weaving. Plenty of small farmers had acquired the craft of walling while working on their holdings and now they could help to balance the budget by contract walling during the quieter seasons of the farming year. Similarly, the village rough mason could always hire himself out as a dyker whenever his stream of contracts dried up. In the longer term, the great new legacy of walls ensured that there would now be permanent employment for a fair number of full-time wallers, who would be engaged in maintaining and repairing the network.

The Parliamentary enclosure walls were not standardised, and in each parish the Commissioners could set their own specification. The height of the walls ranged from just over five feet to six feet, while other differences derived from the local building materials, which could be sandstone, grit or limestone, quarried rock or rounded boulders cleared from the glacial drift in the neighbouring fields. The terms of the award for enclosing the common fields of Linton in Wharfedale have been quoted by the late Dr Raistrick. The Commissioners required walls that were six feet in height, three feet broad at their base and battered to a width of 14 inches at the top. They also demanded that through stones should be included at the rate of 21 per rood (about 5½ yards).

Generally, the beneficiaries of the awards were given just a year to undertake the enclosure of their lands. As a result, each parish must have experienced an unprecedented bustle of activity at the time of enclosure. There may have been gangs of contracted dykers sleeping rough in the laithes or field barns, small quarries being opened on the fell sides to supply the sudden demand for stone, rubble-laden carts and sledges bumping along rutted tracks and rough ground to carry the stone to the dyker's dumps, lime kilns at work to produce the mortar for the top-stones, while all the while the countryside was pervaded by the clatter of hammers. And meanwhile, all the day-to-day work of farming in the Dales could not be neglected.

Enclosure did not only manifest itself in the creation of a new walled fieldscape. As we have seen, it had severe consequences for society in the Dales. For the losers, of whom there were a great many, if often involved migration and the search for a new living in some strange town or foreign land. Life also changed for those who stood to gain from the revolution. Many a farming family had lived in a village or hamlet for generations, treading well-worn tracks to scattered field strips, stream-side meadows and lofty commons. Now, their fragmented holdings in the communal lands were replaced by the award of a compacted block of land, one which might well lie at some distance from the village homestead. Time and again, the decision was taken to abandon the old home, which was so inconveniently distant from the new farm, and to build a new farmstead at the hub of the little farming empire. In the 18th-century this almost invariably took the form of an improved laithe-house. The house and the byre adjoined, but were divided by a continuous wall, the byre being placed on the downslope end of the house for sanitary reasons. Unlike the previous generations of farmsteads, the house was built two storeys tall and was roofed in stone slates rather than thatch, while the windows in the facade were positioned in a symmetrical manner, according to the dictates of current fashion. Enclosure struck the local communities like a great earthquake, consigning some neighbours to the slavery of the mill towns, while elevating others to what must often have been regarded as a rather splendid isolation in a spacious and newly-built farmstead commanding much of the land around.

Enclosure did not end with the creation of new field walls and farmsteads and barns. There was also scope for the provision of new roads. Since the surveyors enjoyed considerable freedom where the old common lands were concerned, these roads were generally designed to run every bit as straight as the field walls on either side. However, there was no danger that the road-

building feats of the Romans would be rivalled. Although the old Forest of Knaresborough, spanning much of Nidderdale, was enclosed in one swoop, enclosure normally operated on a piecemeal parish-by-parish basis. Decades could separate the enclosure of neighbouring parishes, and so it was not possible to create a good system of integrated roads. Attempts to improve the system of transport in the Dales often came to a dead end at the parish boundary and, although the new enclosure roads often improved things at a parochial level, it was the turnpike movement, active at roughly the same time, that did so much to improve communications through the region as a whole.

Visitors arrive to enjoy the scenery of the Dales in ever increasing numbers. As they gaze across views in which everything seems to be in harmony with its setting, many must imagine that they are enjoying an almost timeless scene – one which is quite untouched by the discord and clamour of recent times. It is true that almost every landscape in the Dales has inherited something from prehistoric or medieval times. But there are so many countrysides which are very largely of a Georgian, Regency or early-Victorian vintage. Time and again one sees places where

Stile near Askrigg. *'This is a beautiful piece of work, carved with a hammer and chisel, I'd say. It'd cost a fortune today – £300, I should think, for all the hours put in. Look how it slopes at the top.'*

the fieldscape, with its drystone walls, the straight little roads, the scattered stone farmsteads and their subservient field barns all date from the time of enclosure and its immediate aftermath. These are countrysides where the outlines of the landscape were not the result of a centuries-long evolution. Rather, they were cobbled together by a surveyor and valuer – perhaps working by oil lamp in the local inn after a day of tramping and mapping in the fields around. And then, with a pen and ruler, the old countryside was obliterated and a new one manufactured.

There is nowhere better than the Dales to discover the world as it was viewed through 18th-century eyes. Looking across enclosure countryside one can see the quest for orderliness and for mastery of the setting. Also manifest in the scene is the contempt for the lower strata in society, the belief in property and self betterment: the Protestant work ethic converted into countryside.

And yet the dispossessed commoners and broken smallholders were not the only people who regarded the new order as an affront. Writing in Victorian times, T.D. Whitaker of Threshfield thought that the enclosures ". . . have spoiled the face of the county as an object; the cornfields which by variegated hues of tillage relieved the uniformity of verdure about them are now no more; and the fine swelling outlines of the pastures, formerly as extensive as large parks, and wanting little but the accompaniment

Rowan tree and the south side of Buckden.
'That was taken looking across to the Cray road. Those sheep make it a perfect shot. It's got everything – sky, rocks, sheep...'

are home to rabbits and perching points for wheatears. Unlike the older Victorians, we cannot imagine the countryside of the Dales not being ". . . strapped over with large bandages of stone." From countless vantage points we can see the curving jigsaw pattern of medieval, 16th- and 17th-century walls around the villages and hamlets giving way to the irregular network of intake walls on the lower fell sides, with these patterns yielding in turn to the arrow-straight enclosure walls which slice up the ancient commons without heed to terrain and the lie of the land.

Everything in the scene seems to be just as it should be – and yet we know that the only constant in the landscape story is change itself. During the current evolutionary phase, old walls are being pulled down or allowed to tumble as hill farms fail and amalgamate and as the farmers convert snug little pastures into broader ranges. Where they stand, the walls still do good work, providing sheep with shelter from the wind and driving rain, but a well-maintained network of field walls is often viewed as a luxury which the farmer cannot afford.

Those who travel around the Dales will soon become aware that drystone walling is far from being a forgotten art. There are plenty of professional wallers in the region who have full order books and who are capable of work every bit as good as that which was accomplished by the contract dykers of the enclosure years. One often sees them at work at the roadside. But it is at the roadside that most of the work takes place. It is much rarer to see walling going on deep in the heart of the field network. Indeed, much of the stone which is used to dignify a garden frontage or define the edges of a widened road is recycled from old field walls which were neglected or condemned by the farmer concerned. So often, the stone is more valued as a trailer load than as a wall, and, Dales farmers being the way that they are, it is seldom sold at less than a fair price. Most hill farmers can make a rough and ready job of patching-up a wall section toppled by a raging gale or damaged by thoughtless ramblers, but insurance companies are there to pay-up when a car skids off an icy corner and ploughs through a wall. These little disasters provide a stream of bread and butter work for the professional wallers.

Only time will tell whether the intricate stone tracery of walls will prove to be an enduring feature of the Dales scene. At present, it seems as though two centuries of frantic wall building followed by one of relative stability is being followed by another in which walls will slowly decay. But this is not a region in which predictions can easily be made. In the meantime, let us enjoy the distinctive scenery for as long as we may, paint it, photograph it and tell of its character and charms. And then if the worst befalls there will still be the record and the memory.

of deer to render them as beautiful, are now strapped over with large bandages of stone, and present nothing to the eye but lines and angular deformity."

But with the passing of one or two centuries, the enclosure walls have come to be regarded as an important part of the landscape heritage of the Dales. They are weathered and mellowed by the same elemental forces which dull and soften the dwellings and scars. Now patterned by lichens in pastel shades of orange, white and green, they

A FELLOW OF INFINITE ZEST

By Maurice Colbeck

Geoff Lund likes animals, lamps, photography, music, walling, work and people – most people, that is – and women, perhaps, more than most. With a smile as wide as Wharfedale he greets me at the door of the cottage in Burnsall which he shares with his brother. He looks younger than his sixty-odd years: his hair is still dark and he has the sturdy build you expect in a Dalesman. But it is the openness of his expression that strikes you first. Instantly you sense that what you see before you is what there is to see of Geoff Lund. There is nothing hidden. "If Ah don't take to folk they get nowhere wi' me," he warns you.

I hope he takes to me as, talking all the time, he leads me upstairs to his very own quarters, the attic of the house overlooking the great green where the Wharfe winds by – and opens the door on another world.

This, if I had to name it, I would call Lundland. At least four table lamps shed light through the little room which is crowded with his treasures. He has made the posts of the lamps himself from curiously shaped tree branches picked up here and there. They form centrepieces for scenes he has created by the use of miniature animals. "These lamps are all to do with balance and they're the only ones in the world," he says.

He invites my comments on the animal figures – "Hens do go up trees, don't they? And these are ptarmigan, aren't they? I would have thought so, anyway." Being a gamekeeper's son, he surely knows better than I, but his native courtesy forbids dogmatism.

A pachyderm person myself, I admire Geoff's collection of elephants. "That one's facing the door – are yours?" he enquires with interest. "You should have 'em facing t' door – for luck. . . You see that deer behind you? It's bronze calcium, limited edition. What I've got in mind is to have a big moon coming up very slowly, behind the sofa for instance." The ceiling is studded with little stars which light up magically when he turns off the lights, and shine for forty-five minutes. "I've got enough ornaments now," he says, and has recently gone in for collecting more and more video and audio-tape cassettes, which he plays in a variety of permutations bewildering to the non-technical – like the compensators and pre-focusing of his photography.

All around the walls are enlargements of Geoff's wonderful photographs of the Dales. These are the reason I've come to see him. Having known many photographers, I expect him to talk about little but his pictures and how he took them. Therefore, I am pleasantly surprised.

"Sit in the blue chair – it's the best," he orders hospitably while I'm still introducing myself and my purpose. "Yes, that one – it's a beautiful chair!" Cost him £500 but it was worth it for the sake of his back (a vulnerable spot in a waller). Obediently seated, I ask how he came to take up photography. It happened during his National Service days in Hong Kong with the Royal Artillery. Having seen the unfortunate effects on comrades who had sampled the island's flesh-pots, he decided photography was a safer passion for his off-duty hours.

Until then he had never owned a camera, though from his earliest days as a lad in Malhamdale, where he walked six miles each day to school, he has been enraptured by 'views'. He recalls: "On one beautiful sunny morning, about eight o'clock, there was this mist sat over Malham – a blue mist just sat over it." The excitement in his voice rekindles the vividness of that boyhood experience, as he adds. . . "It's things like that that spark you off."

Geoff was born at Malham Tarn – the last of ten children of a mole-catcher. There were twelve in

Below Scargill, looking towards Kettlewell.

all, but two died at birth. "I weighed eleven pound and brother John, who lives below, weighed twelve. My mother had breast-fed nine, but one missed, and he lost all his teeth before he was twenty-six. I haven't had toothache in my life and I've still got all my teeth. That's calcium, isn't it?"

He has a way of inviting your agreement as if he assumes you know at least as much as he does, whether the subject be music, photography, printing or the flora and fauna of the Dales. "Folk'll say I'm a know-all," he apologises cheerfully, after holding forth on one or other of the above. But whatever Geoff is, he isn't that. "You're an enthusiast," I tell him. He considers this briefly before telling me more about his father.

Lund senior, after a spell as a farm-worker, became a gamekeeper. "He was an incredible shot, but he never boasted about it. And then he became a mole-catcher. He caught two white moles every year at Foxup, in the same place – two! – until he'd got enough to make my mother a pair of gloves – I think it took about sixteen. He could skin a mole in about nineteen seconds – he had a big long knife. And then he'd put the skins on a board and send 'em to Horace and Friends, who bought 'em for twopence or threepence."

On leaving school, Geoff, like most young Dalesmen, worked for a time on the land. "I was a farm-worker in Littondale until I got sick of it. I couldn't stand the dust. I sneezed till dinnertime! So I went into a bakery at Skipton, but after a month there I couldn't stand the heat. I went on the railway because I'd always wanted to be an engine-driver – little did they tell you you'd be fifty before you got there!" He had started as a locomotive cleaner at two pounds and sixpence a week. During a blizzard he was called out as one of a gang to dig a train out of the snow at Aisgill – "which as you know is the highest point on the Settle-Carlisle line.

"There stood the engine, with its firebox that I'd cleaned out only a week before. I was amazed! I wish I'd had a camera in them days because the train, which was pushing a snowplough, pulled up from a tremendous speed when it hit an enormous drift. It was a brilliant sight. . ."

With some satisfaction, Geoff recalls: "I got six pounds nineteen that week." But, welcome though it was, it was not enough to keep him on any railway where it took so long to become an engine-driver. He went back to farm work, then in 1947, took up walling.

According to Geoff, it was 'defiance' that made him decide to stay with that craft. On one occasion someone else, Geoff felt, had taken the credit for a particularly fine bit of his work and this made him determined to show what he could really do as a waller if he set his mind to it. The lines of his destiny were converging – and lines are important in Geoff's philosophy. Photography and walling, he says now, are "pretty much the same thing if you have the artistic temperament and an eye for the line an' that." This has something to do with the reason bridges fascinate him. "You can't go wrong with a bridge," he says, presumably thinking of photography, though everyday objects can lead with surprising ease into discussions of his philosophy and weighty questions of good and evil.

By way of farm-work, the railways, walling and photography we suddenly arrive back in Hong Kong, where Geoff tried his prentice hand at photography. His first subjects were views from the heights of the island. Briefly he 'went in for video' but found it hadn't the same appeal as still photography, and he quickly returned to the first love which is now the enduring joy of his life.

Taking pictures occupies most of his time. "At my age, if it's a beautiful day I take pictures instead of walling." But walling, together with allied occupations such as laying setts, is still his main source of income. "I laid some for the Editor of the *Dalesman*, Mr Joy, whilst he was in America. Anything like that I find interesting," he says, as if interest, rather than profit, naturally determines his choice.

"It's a heavy job, though, walling. If a man walls five square yards a day it means he's handled five tons of stone – that's quite a lot in a year. My arms are beginning to wear out – my elbows, anyway." So far, however, there seems to be nothing wrong with his legs and he takes an impish delight in walking unsuspecting visitors off their feet.

For an engine-driver manqué he retains an unsoured love of 'puffer-trains'. Once a month in summer he visits Dentdale, where the towering Aisgill viaduct and its fellow titans of the Settle-Carlisle line induce feelings of awe. But smaller things, too, make him take out the camera that he rarely leaves at home – things like lambs and ducks and the tup sales at Hawes. When a car got in the way as Geoff was trying to take pictures of a flock of sheep crossing a bridge as they were brought down from Malham Moor, a farmer surprised him by rounding up the sheep with his dog and spending several minutes helping him re-stage the shot. "It was so kind of him!" exclaims Geoff, quite unaware that he is the sort of chap even farmers go out of their way to help.

We decide the time has come to show me his slides. We struggle with his screen and folding slide table, which behave rather like demented deckchairs in the limited space. I narrowly avoid sitting on his glasses while we're searching for his projector, but eventually all is ready and the show begins – commentary by Geoff Lund.

"The thing about that picture that's so incredible,"

Waterfall at Bishopdale.

he says of a pattern of outcropping limestone, "is this cross." True enough, though I hadn't seen it, the gleaming rocks form an almost symmetrical diagonal cross. "I waited an hour for the sun to come out to get that."

Geoff, fortunate man, confesses to being fascinated by any number of things, but "absolutely crazy" about waterfalls. Being myself the merest tyro with a camera, though for years a close onlooker at the game, I would say few subjects impose a sterner test on the landscape photographer than white water cascading through a Dales gill in spate. It's a test that Geoff, completely self-taught, passes with honours.

Between slides he tells me about his family. The brother who lives below was a chef ("brilliant at roast duckling") at Burnsall's Red Lion Inn for over forty years. "Now he's gone back to pegging rugs – he gets about seventy quid for one. My sister's clever" – she made Geoff the stuffed hippo snoozing beside his chair, as well as the shades on his lamps. Another brother is a keeper with a deep knowledge of foxes and their ways. He (fortunately) can tell the difference between a rabbit and a polecat by touch in the dark of a wooden box rabbit trap. Yet another sister "goes in for making little old-fashioned dolls – she's very clever too." And he has another sister at Skipton, while his brother Denis farms in Littondale, and another brother, who's something of a motor-cycle ace ("came fifth behind Agostini in the fifties"), lives in the Isle of Man. Yet another brother died of sun-stroke out

**Highland cattle
at Barbondale.**

*'That's between
Kirkby Lonsdale
and Gawthrop, on
the way to
Dentdale. I climbed
that hill the other
week. I thought I
should soon be at
the top, but it was
terrible – I could
have done with
some crampons!
I think those
Highland cattle are
fantastic – they
certainly add to the
view. Ferocious?
They can be.'*

he explains, "because it's a bridge." We move on. "Lovely and bent, those rails, aren't they? . . . Ah! Now I got into the river to get that. . . This is Barbondale." I have to admit I've never heard of it. "It goes from Kirkby Lonsdale to Dentdale," Geoff tells me. Now we're looking at a picture of bracken – he's less happy about this one. "It didn't bring out the depth, and there's such a tremendous depth. So next time, when the sun allows it, I'll have to be right on the very top and look down into that valley. That's the road going over into Dentdale and those hills in the background are Garsdale Head. Oh, now those caves are near Settle. That's Ingleton looking over the top."

The hills are speckled with the lightest powdering of snow – "a covering of flour," Geoff calls it, and for once he seems quite satisfied. "It's a lovely shot is that." This is the first time he has seen these recent shots enlarged by the projector. He is on a voyage of discovery whose excitement he wants to share.

"Ah! Now I like that," he exclaims as a small herd of Highland cattle, their long hair as brown as the bracken, emerge on the screen. "That one's asking what the hell I'm doin'?" Click. Now we see a shot of Grimwith Reservoir, on which "a little straight line" intrigues him mightily. He feels his gift as a photographer is an eye for 'balance', which is enhanced by modern technology – "We're a team! It's all I live for."

Geoff brings me a silver tray holding a huge mug of coffee and a sandwich containing roughly half a chicken. As I eat he demonstrates his hi-fi reproduction of wild life videos. The ghostly cry of a lemur echoes from somewhere near the ceiling. He follows this with a tape he warns me will be pretty powerful. This is disc number five – Ivan Rebroff, a Russian bass who can span five octaves. "Marvellous voice!" says Geoff. Ivan climbs from basso profundo to soaring falsetto as the balalaikes tinkle. Powerful indeed! I mention Chaliapin, and with undiminished eagerness he asks me to write the name down for his future attention. He presses another button on the disc player and the room is resonant with Winifred Atwell.

Geoff's company is both stimulating and tranquilising as he makes you peer through camera lenses in the endless effort to share with you the world he sees. I could have stayed all day, enclosed in his zestful company, but he had some walling to finish – "an' Ah want to photograph an unusual hinge on a gate. Ah've taken one picture of it already, but it's not right." (If I know owt, the problem is bound to be summat to do with straight lines.)

Inevitably, being the character he is, Geoff has been seen now and then on television and heard on radio, but fame will never go to his head. In the Dales, where 'graft' means hard work and not dishonesty, they call him "the little grafter". He's not so little, but the name suits him well enough – perhaps because it rhymes with laughter, something else he's good at.

east during the war.

"What have *you* got?" he suddenly asks me, rather disconcertingly. I realise that of course he's talking about cameras and manage to remember that mine's a Pentax, bought for me by the family because it makes everything so easy. But now we're back with the slides. Gordale Scar appears on the screen, while Geoff is explaining why some folk say he's a loner. "I couldn't possibly find interest in a crowd of people. I talk to myself. I ramble on and argue with myself – You're wrong, I'll say." He chuckles at his foibles.

"I'll just switch that light off behind you." We close a door and position my chair to the best possible advantage. "What's wrong with the light? Something's gone wrong. . ." The picture on the screen has a definite list to starboard. I ease a couple of books under the projector and Geoff is satisfied. "Right! We're away to the woods. . ." What appears to be a double exposure appears on the screen. "That's incredible – I've never seen anything like that. . . I'm having some trouble trying to show you these pictures," he apologises, but the problems are soon overcome and we proceed.

"Don't forget, I was on fifteenth-of-a-second there, hand-held. . . Do you think I'd be better on a twenty-fifth?" I begin protesting that my photographic ignorance is as near bottomless as Malham Tarn itself, but we're already on another slide. "That's an incredible rock," he says. "Ah! Now look at that water going through – have you been to Gordale Scar?" Another slide clicks in place. "Do you like that valley with the tree above it, standing out in the blue sky?

"That's Beck Hall at Malham. And that's the bridge. I'm always looking for perfection – I hate straight lines, but these straight lines are different,"

STONE WALLS & STILES

Gate at Conistone.
'Somebody's drilled those gateposts and put the hinges in with a little lead pan, and then they've hung the gate on. It saved them putting up a gatepost. Those stones came from just where they were working.'

Gate near Arncliffe. *'This white limestone gatepost is leaning with age – it might have been put up in the eighteenth century.'*

Back of Gordale Scar – *'with the morning sun casting shadows. I took that about half-past twelve, judging by the way the shadow's just moving over. It was the effect of the shadow on the limestone I was after there, though I hadn't set out at first with that in mind.'*

Looking towards Scargill and Kettlewell.

Stile near Leyburn. *'That's a real farmer's stile and whoever built it must have had thin legs! The little fat gatepost on the left is leaning towards us quite a bit, though it doesn't show much on the picture. There's a lot of difference between the two stones – they're like cheese and chalk.'*

Gatepost on Deadman's Hill, between Kettlewell and Kilnsey. *'I don't know how the hill got its name. There's a legend, of course, that somebody was killed on it. The hole in that gatepost is natural, I'm sure – I don't think anybody put it there. These yellow flowers are called "dogstanders". Farmers hate them because they're no use to the animals – they eat round them.'*

Stone troughs at Howgill Lodge.
'They're sat on the side of the road for horses and they'd be put there to catch the water from a little natural stream coming through that square. Don't know why there are two troughs, though you often see two together. One would run into the other.'

Stile at Askrigg, framing the view towards Swaledale. *'It's a marvellous stile, though there are many versions of it. Must have taken time to build, as well as natural ability, to get the slant right: I think he'd put his stones on the ground first to try 'em out.'*

Wooden stiles below Pen-y-ghent. *'I'd been on the top of Pen-y-ghent in the mist to take pictures. All the valley had been covered in mist that day. If I'd shot sooner I'd have had the mist sweeping across Pen-y-ghent. I often go up there, but you have to be dressed for it. The cold can be fatal sometimes.'*

Two stone sheep pens.

Stile at Askrigg.

Back road to Conistone with hawthorn tree red with berries.

View from west of Arncliffe. *'I was trying to get these field walls again. I don't like that slant of the hill, but the picture's fairly well balanced and the trees helped. It's a nice tranquil scene.'*

RIVERS & WATERFALLS

Waterfall on the Wharfe below Kilnsey. *'I'm absolutely fascinated by water and waterfalls, because there are so many different angles.'*

Waterfall in Bishopdale. *'The beck here dries up, except for a trickle, between floods. It's the old story of limestone again; it's porous and there are deep cracks in it, so it doesn't hold the water. You hear of underground lakes an' that.'*

Icicles on waterfall at Buckden Gill under Buckden Pike. *'You often see that in winter, but with this global warming, it happens less often — there wasn't much of a frost this winter at all.'*

Crystal Beck, Littondale, after ground frost.
'There'd been a thick fog that morning and you can still see some of it hanging about. It cleared about half-past two.'

Packhorse bridge, Foxup, on the road to Cosh.
'There's one of the loneliest farmhouses in Britain at Cosh. One winter the people there hadn't been seen for a week, so my brother got his horse out and went to look for 'em in a big snowstorm. He couldn't even find t' house! This is a bad job, he thought, so he set off home – and his horse put its foot down t' chimney. True story? No, it's myth! But for the last three-quarters of a mile you can't see the house, it's so hidden away.'

Clear water below Kettlewell school. *'That's an incredibly clear picture! And that water – I could see the insects at the bottom.'*

**Starbotton Gill
with waterfall.**

Tree and stream below Janet's Foss at Gordale Scar. *'I'm my own severest critic. I think that I should have taken a little bit more of the tree. Half an inch would have made all the difference in the world.'*

47

Stream near Mossdale Cavern.
'Absolutely beautiful, that, isn't it? At Mossdale Cavern some years ago there was a pot-holing tragedy. That was a very different sort of day... Ominous... You could tell something was going to happen, and when it did, the stream overflowed, water poured in and there was nothing could be done. There's a plaque to the victims of the tragedy in Conistone church.'

Opposite: 'Gossamer' waterfall, Valley of Desolation.

Bishopdale from behind the waterfall. *'I'd two slides on my camera to take the picture on print as well as slide. I came out to take another shot, but the camera wouldn't work. I guessed I'd got some moisture on two electrical contacts, so I rubbed them dry and it worked.'*

Buckden Gill waterfall. *'This is a favourite of mine. I had to work very hard to avoid putting that rock in line with the waterfall. I moved this way and that way until I got it, and that picture is as perfectly balanced now as I could ever get it.'*

51

Waterfall below Kilnsey. *'That cloud's called Tony – cause it's t' on'y cloud there is.'*

Gill in Bishopdale.
'Another of these little valleys you find as you go down.'

**The top of
Buckden Gill.**
*'That shot has a
perfection for me
and that sheep
helped to make it for
me by walking
across. Lovely, isn't
it? I like to get
animals in my
pictures.'*

Desolation Valley. *'Now then, what's wrong with that picture? I'll tell you: those two damn stones seem to stick out – they're too symmetrical.'*

Starbotton Gill.
'That is beautiful. I lost my slide there, the one I use to change camera backs from print to slide. I eventually found it among the rushes on the left of the picture. It was standing upright or I'd have seen it shining. I lost one again the other day and had to buy another – fourteen quid!'

Waterfall, Valley of Desolation. *'In winter you can't do a very good job of photographing this because there's a hillock behind me that stops the sun coming on.'*

57

Below Loup Scar on the river at Burnsall. *'When I was in my early teens I was on there with two other lads in a leaky boat. The water's twelve or fifteen foot deep, but none of us could swim and we'd to keep bailing the water out. How stupid and dangerous it was! And we're all three still living to this day.'*

Frosty morning in Buckden Gill.

**Bishopdale:
waterfall in
autumn.**

Waterfall in Starbotton Gill. *'What can I say about that? Nothing, except that it's a beautiful little stream which not many people see, because there's no footpath.'*

FARMING

Walter Walker, of Appletreewick, feeding a pet lamb. *'Our Walter's a great character! Virtually eighty years old and still working. A marvellous sheep man with his Scotch tups is Walter. The Walkers are a large farming family all round the dale and all hard workers.'*

Scotch tups owned by Walter Walker.

Walter Walker ruddles a tup, with his son Patrick. *'They've got a red week, a blue week and one without. When the ewe is mated, the farmer will know by looking at its back when it was mated and when it will be likely to have its lambs.'*

Tree skeleton near Thorpe Lane end. *'I was there to photograph sheep, but what has made this shot fantastic is the tree. It's only come to me in the last few years, but now I certainly enjoy taking pictures of trees when the branches are bare of leaves.'*

Walter Walker shearing. *'He's using an old-fashioned stock which was also used at one time for killing pigs – it was a brutal, cruel way to do it! I hated it even as a boy. The pig was tied up and it would scream for ages before and during the act. They used to stick a knife into the jugular vein, with a bucket underneath to catch the blood for making black puddings.'*

**Calves among
the thistles at
Malham.** *'Have
you ever seen
thistles this big?'*

Sheep feeding in winter at Bishopdale.

Dalesbred sheep. *'Look at them two little white patches at t' side of his nose – that's how you tell a Dalesbred. I took the picture because of the beautiful background and to show what a Dalesbred sheep looks like. This is a beauty.'*

Woodland sheep.
*'Woodlands are a
rare breed. They
look like mountain
goats on that piece
of natural rock
above Kettlewell.'*

Scotch tup on a foggy morning at Litton. *'He followed me and just stood there on Belger track and I couldn't resist him. He was hoping for a handout, I suppose, but I'd nothing to give him.'*

Sheep above Grimwith. *'This is our Walter again and his sheep above Grimwith reservoir. He wanted me to film them here because of the lake in the background.'*

Conistone-with-Kilnsey. *'It's called that because, if you say "Conistone" only, you could be taken to mean the one near Hellifield.'*

Gordon Sutcliffe carting hay to his sheep.

Bantam mum and family. *'That one was taken back o' Broadshaw, which had not been lived in for thirty years until some people from Sheffield moved in.'*

Chain gang. *'These tups have been chained together to stop them fighting. Tups of other breeds have longer legs than the Scotch tups, so what happens? The two tups charge and the Scotch tup hits the nose of the other and breaks his neck – crack, bang – because he's lower. Scotch tups have horns and they're rock-hard. These two are Swaledales, but they're chained as well, because all tups fight.'*

Highland cattle in Barbondale.

Mist near Halton East.

LANDSCAPES & PEAKS

Misty valleys below Pen-y-ghent.

Dry beck above Gordale Scar.
'That is a stupendous picture all round, taken on the way from Gordale Scar to Malham Tarn.'

Frosted hawthorn tree near Litton. *'Just happened to see it as I was passing so I thought, I must have that.'*

Rock on Plover Hill near Foxup.
'I was coming home when I took that at the end of the day. Don't know how that rock got there. Must have been a glacier that brought it.'

Basin with mist.
'I was extremely pleased with this because you can see as far as Wild Boar Fell.'

**Below
Appletreewick,
near the New Inn.**
*'I had to wait half an
hour for the clouds
to move there.'*

Rock formation.
'I didn't go looking for that rock. I just happened to be walking towards the road above Malham when I saw it. It was incredible. Don't ask me what kind of rock it is, I'm baffled — you'll have to ask Richard Muir about that.'

Mist over Buckden. *'I only took that because I didn't want to miss the mist!'*

Stone sentinel above Cray.

Looking towards Appletreewick with Simon's Seat behind.

Burnsall, looking up Wharfedale. *'You can see Great Whernside, you can see Buckden Pike. It's an incredible picture for depth of field.'*

Grassington from Robin Hood's Quarry, near Netherside. *'It was the view across to Grassington that attracted me. You can't take many shots of Grassington really. I got the river and the road together there.'*

Grimwith reservoir. *'It was a most remarkable day. It isn't often one gets a still surface at Grimwith.'*

Rock formation
above Stake Pass,
near Cray.

Tree in rock formation, Malham. *'When I was a boy, we used to look down those cracks in the limestone for rabbits which had crept into them, thinking they were safe. We'd use a long piece of wire to fetch one out. I wouldn't do it now, it was cruel.'*

Rock formation, Gordale Scar.
'It was one of those beautiful days when I got through a lot of shots.'

On the way to Black Park. *'That rock's worshipped by the redskins! It's like a totem pole or something on Easter Island.'*

Above Robin Hood's Quarry near Netherside.

On the road to Coverdale. *'I'd to take the topstones off the wall to get that shot or the sun would have been into my lens — I put 'em back.'*

Ramblers
descending
Pen-y-ghent.

**Gouthwaite
Reservoir from
the hill above
Pateley.** *'But don't
ask me its name!'*

Holly tree near Burnsall *'with Gill's farm in the foreground.'*

Looking down pathway to Gordale Scar.
'That was difficult because the sun was facing me. I had to wait till three o'clock... A very atmospheric place.'

**On the way to
Mossdale.**

Near Starbotton. *'That's a rock formation that intrigues me. I know I've got a straight line between those two trees but it was the only way I could get the rock formation. I don't like straight lines because there's hardly anything straight in this world!'*

Morning mist near Kettlewell. *'I set off to photograph a hot-air balloon, but I ended up with this mist. Beautiful, isn't it?'*

Up Buckden Gill.
'Very difficult to photograph in winter, because the sun never leaves that side.'

Sunset over Grimwith reservoir. *'That reminds me of the symmetrical effects you get from paper-tearing acts on the stage. I stood dead-centre to take it and that's the result. I'd love to have had a red sun though.'*

FLORA

Flowers at Harrogate. *'I don't know why they have a flower show there because you've got it good enough as it is!'*

Bluebells in the Valley of Desolation. *'I took that because the bluebells face up to a little hillock, and because they're partly in the shadow and because of that tree leaning over. That picture has a perfect balance: the arch of the bough is over the arch of the bluebells – and those leaves on the left are beautiful.'*

Garden at
Arncliffe.

Daffodils at
Barden.

Ash tree at Hole Bottom, Hebden.
'That is the beginning of my photographing trees. I saw it silhouetted against the blue sky and I thought, that's incredible!'

Hawthorn tree near Wath. *'I"ve never seen berries like that in my life, except in 1990. That tree's absolutely covered.'*

Bluebells above Catgill Farm, Bolton Abbey.

BUILDINGS & BRIDGES

**'Miners' Bridge',
Hebden Gill.** *'It's
beautiful the way
they've walled into
that arch. Not one o'
mine – I'd be an old
chap now if it was!'*

Train on a viaduct in Dentdale. *'That's taken from an angle I've never seen before. I think it's being born in the countryside that gives you an ability to spot views. But it was photography that brought it out in me.'*

Arten Gill viaduct. *'This is the topside of the viaduct, looking right down Dentdale. I particularly like the little shafts of light where the arches come through.'*

Barn near Hawes,
  Wensleydale.

Derelict house overlooking Coverdale. *'It hasn't been lived in in my time. Mebbe it was once lived in by a shepherd. There's a round fence in front of it where they must have kept sheep.'*

Ling-burning
above Grimwith
reservoir.

Early morning
reflections,
Burnsall Bridge.

Stone doorway at Deepdale dated 1668.

Stone bridge at Malham Cove.
'I've never before seen that bridge on a photograph with Malham Cove, and I can't understand why.'

Thatched building at Grimwith reservoir. *'They came from the south of England to thatch that, because nobody up here could do it.'*

Derelict barn above Wath. *'It's disappearing into the past – that's why I took it. I like the leaning gateposts in the foreground – they've had their chips, they're on their way out!'*

Early morning at Burnsall Bridge.
'There's only you and the ducks — they've been fed on bread from the Red Lion for years. Bridge of sighs, I call it. Why? I don't know — because it's so beautiful. That view's admired far and wide.'

Steam train crossing Denthead viaduct on the Settle-Carlisle line. *'One reason for taking that was the little farmhouse you can see through one arch. I maybe should have waited a little longer: I'd like to have had the train more central.'*

Swaledale barn hiding view of Gunnerside. *'There's been another little building there, but don't ask me what. Now only the stones are left and the sheep were just wandering in and out of that.'*

Keeper's building near Angram. *'I presume this is where the people stop for a meal when they're driving birds on a shoot. I don't know much about it – it's certainly colourful.'*

Viaduct in Dentdale. *'That's a beautiful shot, I think. This is the first viaduct you see when you go down into Dentdale. Why do I like it? Well, the road's in shadow, as it should be, and you get a hell of a lot of hills in there.'*

SNOW SCENES

**Below Burnsall
on the way to
Appletreewick.**
*'I'd seen this view a
week before, but I'd
been photographing
up-dale and tore
down in my car at
high speed just to
get there in time for
the sun to be just
right.'*

Footprints in the snow. *'One of my great favourites and those are my feetmarks in the foreground – size nine! This is a very rare picture of the two valleys, Buckdendale and Littondale, and the only reason I came to shoot it was that somebody wanted a shot of their farm at the bottom under Kilnsey Crag. I had to wait for three-quarters of an hour for the wall of cloud to move to one side.'*

Bolton Abbey estate from Simon's Seat. *'I'm not a great lover of this, because I've got a white line in front and I shouldn't have done. I should have pushed that to one side and gone nearer those trees. I had one of the hardest walks I've ever had, to get there, the snow was so deep.'*

Starbotton from a hill above Kettlewell. *'I'd like to go back there in summer – and might get the farmer to put his sheep and cows in front.'*

Gateway on Park Rash. *'This was taken after a spectacular snowstorm. You're looking down towards Cracoe. Park Rash farmhouse is in those trees on the right.'*

Towards Simon's Seat from Barden.
'I took this because I thought that tree had broken off with the weight of the snow. I like the way all those trees are covered with that plastered snow.'

Footbridge, Hebden Gill. *'The people on the bridge are in the wrong place, if they'd been a foot nearer me they would have been perfect.'*

Arncliffe in the snow. *'That sign tells you you're coming into one of the most beautiful villages I've ever worked in. It's so tranquil and you can see the rolling hills.'*

Arncliffe church.
*'I made a mistake
with this. I got the
tree branches
coming down on to
the church top and
I shouldn't have
done. I should have
walked up a few
feet.'*

Early morning, Kilnsey. *'I stopped at the top of Deadman's Hill and then I saw these sheep all sitting in the sun asleep. I nipped round to get them from the back looking out, then a car pulled up at the gate and they all rushed off to see if he'd brought some hay. I was a bit annoyed, but it turned out to be a beautiful shot as it is.'*

Sunrise, Lower Dock, Barden. *'That sweep of tyre-marks is beautiful, when you look. You've straight lines, curves and triangles there.'*

Burnsall in the snow. *'I live in Burnsall. It's a beautiful place, though it's in gritstone country and I'm a limestone man. I love Malham Tarn, where I was born, I love Malham. I love it all round here, but if you gave me the choice, I'd opt for limestone country.'*

Below Arncliffe church. *'There was a very strange light that morning and all the pictures I took were beautiful. The balance of that one is wonderful with that beautiful arched tree.'*

Pen-y-ghent from Neil's Ing.
'There were so many things to choose from here. I made use of those rushes to fill the foreground. You can see Neil's Ing in the trees on your right.'

Below Hebden swing bridge. *'I took that about nine or ten o'clock. The tree won't be here in two years' time because it's got Dutch elm disease.'*

Blea Gill near Grimwith reservoir. *'That's what they call a smattering of snow.'*

Darnbrook Gill.
'Not one of my favourites – too much shadow.'

**Kettlewelldale,
early spring.**

**Springs Wood,
Litton, in winter.**
*'A peach of a
picture! I like the
shape of the trees,
but what I love most
of all is the snow on
top of the branches.'*

The walk to Buckden Pike after a storm.
'It's a lovely walk. The walls are falling away, but that's what's happening to these Dales walls – so many of them are going.'